The Ultimate
Elephant
Book for Kids

100+ Amazing Elephant Facts, Photos & More

Jenny Kellett

BELLANOVA

MELBOURNE · SOFIA · BERLIN

www.bellanovabooks.com

Copyright © 2023 by Jenny Kellett

ISBN: 978-619-264-027-9
Imprint: Bellanova Books

CONTENTS

INTRODUCTION

It's hard not to love elephants! But how much do you really know about your favorite animal? Don't worry, you'll be an elephant expert in no time!

In this book you will learn over 100 amazing new things about the world's largest land mammal. Then, test your knowledge in the quiz.

Are you ready? *Let's go!*

An African
elephant.

ELEPHANT SPECIES

Elephants are some of the most majestic and fascinating creatures on Earth! Did you know that there are actually three different types of elephants?

Sadly, all three species of elephants are endangered and are facing threats such as habitat loss and poaching. But we can all do our part to help protect these amazing creatures.

Let's take a closer look at the differences between them.

An Asian elephant.

AFRICAN BUSH ELEPHANT

The African bush elephant (**Loxodonta africana)** is the giant of the elephant world! They can weigh up to 10 tons and are the biggest land animals on Earth. You'll recognize them by their huge ears that they use like air conditioning to cool off on hot days.

They live in 37 different sub-Saharan African countries, including Uganda, Tanzania, Kenya and Zambia.

African bush
elephants are
happy living in a
variety of habitats
including forests,
grasslands, wetlands and
agricultural land.

They don't like being alone. This species is very social, living in small groups or herds of either bulls or cows.

African bush elephants are wrinklier than African forest elephants, which helps them keep much-needed water close to their skin. And when it comes to tusks, these elephants are the strongmen of the herd, with big, long tusks that are used for heavy lifting.

The African bush elephant is listed as **endangered** on the IUCN Red List, meaning it is very likely to become extinct in the future if things don't change.

AFRICAN FOREST ELEPHANT

African forest elephants (***Loxodonta cyclotis***) are a subspecies of the African elephant and are found in the dense rainforests of Central and West Africa. They are smaller than their savannah-dwelling cousins, and have straighter, downward-pointing tusks that are used for cutting down trees and stripping bark. They have a more reddish color, smaller ears, and a more rounded forehead.

Unlike the African bush elephant, they are elusive and shy, making them difficult to study and photograph. They live in tight-knit family groups led by matriarchs and spend most of their time deep in the forest, where they play an important role in shaping the forest ecosystem.

Unfortunately, African forest elephants are **critically endangered**, with their population declining by over 60% in the past decade due to habitat loss and poaching for their valuable ivory tusks. Unless we work to save them, they could disappear forever.

ASIAN ELEPHANT

The Asian elephant (*Elephas maximus*), also known as the Indian elephant, is a species of elephant found only in Asia. It is the largest land animal in Asia and is smaller than the African elephant. They are typically gray in color and have smaller ears compared to the African elephant.

They are also known for having a distinct, multi-fingerlike projection at the tip of their trunk, which is used for grasping and moving objects.

Asian elephants live in a variety of
habitats, including rainforests, grasslands,
and wetlands, and they are found in 13
countries in Asia, including India, Sri Lanka,
Indonesia, and Malaysia.

They are herbivores and eat a wide variety of plants, including grasses, fruits, and tree bark.

Asian elephants are social animals and live in herds led by a dominant female, known as the matriarch. They have a complex social structure and use a variety of vocalizations, including trumpeting, to communicate with each other.

Asian elephants are considered to be an **endangered** species, with their population estimated to be around 35,000-50,000 in the wild. Habitat loss, poaching for their ivory tusks, and human-elephant conflict are the major threats to their survival.

ELEPHANT FACTS

Elephants are known for their long lifespan, with the potential to live for over 70 years in the wild. In captivity, elephants may live even longer as they are protected from predators and disease.

• • •

When it comes to heartbeats, elephants are the picture of calm and steady. Their pulse rate is around 27 beats per minute. Compare this to a canary's pulse of 1,000 beats per minute.

Just like humans are left-handed or right-handed, elephants prefer one tusk over the other.

• • •

Elephants are the only mammals that can't jump. But are you surprised?

• • •

The skin of an elephant is an inch (2.5 cm) thick.

• • •

Although elephants have poor eyesight, they have a very good sense of smell.

An African
elephant.

Elephants make a noise similar to a cat's purr. These low-frequency sounds can't be heard by humans, but they can travel long distances through the ground and can be picked up by other elephant's feet and trunks.

Elephants' tusks are used for lots of things, including lifting, digging for water and protecting themselves against attackers.

• • •

There are more than 40,000 muscles inside an elephant's trunk! These muscles give their trunks a lot of strength and flexibility.

• • •

Elephants are very friendly—they often wrap their trunks around another elephant's trunk as a way of hugging them.

Have you ever seen an elephant wave its trunk side-to-side and up and down? They do this to improve their sense of smell.

• • •

Elephants have the longest pregnancies of all animals. From conception, it is 22 months until birth!

• • •

An elephant's trunk can do lots of cool things. It can sense the size, shape and temperature of an object. They can also use their trunks to lift up food and suck up water, which they then put in their mouths.

Elephants are excellent swimmers and they use their trunks as a snorkel to breathe while they are in the water. This ability allows them to cross rivers, lakes and other bodies of water with ease, and enables them to reach food sources and escape from predators that cannot swim.

• • •

Despite their size, elephants can be almost silent when they walk thanks to padding on their feet.

• • •

In just one day, an elephant can drink 80 gallons (300 litres) of water!

Elephants are very intelligent. They are known to have good memory, problem-solving skills, and the ability to use tools.

• • •

The elephant is the national animal of Thailand.

• • •

An elephant's trunk can hold up to two gallons (7.5 l) of water.

• • •

Just one elephant tooth can weigh up to 6.6 lb (3 kg)!

An African elephant and
her calf.

Elephants are the world's largest land mammal, with adult males growing up to 4 meters (13 ft) in height and weighing between 5,500-6,600 kg (12,000-14,500 lbs).

• • •

Elephants can smell water from three miles (4.8 km) away!

• • •

The average walking speed of an elephant is around 3-4 miles per hour (5-6 km/h). However, African elephants can run up to 25 mp/h (40 km/h) if they need to!

An African
elephant.

An African
elephant.

Elephants possess the largest brain of any land animal, and among the largest of all animals. An adult elephant's brain weighs around 5 kg (11 lb), which is about 2.5 times larger than the brain of a human!

• • •

Elephants spend 16 hours of each day eating!

• • •

Elephant **calves** (baby elephants) often suck their own trunks for comfort, just like humans suck their thumbs.

Elephants have large ears that they use for lots of purposes, one of which is to keep themselves cool. When elephants are hot, they flap their ears to create a breeze that cools their blood vessels in the ear, which in turn cools down their entire body.

• • •

Elephants' trunks keep growing their entire lives.

• • •

Elephants have no natural predators — only humans hunt them.

An Asian
elephant.

Elephants only sleep two hours a day.

• • •

Elephants have very sensitive skin — they can even feel when a fly lands on them.

• • •

Adult male elephants are called **bulls**. Adult female elephants are called **cows**.

• • •

Male elephants leave their herd when they are around 12-15 years old.

African elephants in
their natural habitat.

Elephants are **herbivores**, meaning they only eat plants. They can eat as much as 300-600 lbs (136-272 kg) of vegetation per day, depending on the type of vegetation available.

• • •

Elephants do not have sweat glands.

• • •

Elephants usually live in tight social groups, called **herds**, which are led by a matriarch.

• • •

Elephants can recognize themselves in the mirror — most animals can not.

An Asian elephant
and her calf.

Elephants can get sunburnt, but they're smart and look after their skin by pouring sand over themselves.

• • •

Elephants haven't always been called that. Before the 14th century, we called them '**oliphants**'.

• • •

Baby elephants are cared for by their mothers, but also by other females in the herd, which are called **aunties**.

An African
elephant calf.

Elephants replace their teeth six times over a lifetime.

• • •

Female elephants usually have their first calf when they are between 10 and 20 years old.

• • •

Elephants play a vital role in the ecosystem by helping to spread seeds and shape the environment through their feeding behaviors. They can knock down trees and trample through dense underbrush, creating pathways for other animals and helping to promote the growth of new vegetation.

An African elephants' tusks can reach over 10 feet (3 m) in length! However, the length and size of an elephant's tusk depends on both genetics and diet.

• • •

The scientific name for the species of African elephants is *Loxodonta*.

• • •

The scientific name for Asian elephants is *Elephas Maximus*.

< **An African bush elephant.**

Elephants only live in the wild in Africa and Asia.

• • •

Elephants weigh between 120 to 165 pounds (54 to 75 kg) when they are born.

• • •

Male elephants go through states called 'musth', which are short periods of madness. During musth, a male elephant's testosterone levels are significantly elevated, which can cause aggression.

**An African
elephant calf.**

It is extremely rare for elephants to have twins; they almost always just have one calf at a time.

• • •

Female elephants usually stop having calves when they are around 50 years old.

• • •

When an elephant dies, the rest of its herd goes into mourning. They will often sit with the body for days.

Elephants don't digest their food very well — there are often whole plants and twigs in their poo!

. . .

Although elephants are generally very gentle animals, they have been known to attack humans if they are provoked.

. . .

When born, elephant calves are almost completely blind. They rely on their elders and their trunks to help them navigate around.

A herd of African elephants.

In many Asian cultures, elephants represent a symbol of wisdom.

• • •

When an elephant is angry, it waves its trunk around and throws mud into the air.

The oldest elephant on record was named Lin Wang and was an Asian elephant who lived in Taiwan. He was born in the wild in 1918, and was captured and brought to the Taipei Zoo in Taiwan in 1951. He lived there for the rest of his life, passing away in 2003 at the age of 85 years old.

• • •

Elephants have been on Earth for over two million years.

• • •

Asian elephants have one finger-like projection at the tip of their trunks, which is useful for holding things. African elephants, on the other hand, have two 'fingers'.

When an elephant herd feels threatened, the adult elephants will form a protective circle around the calves.

• • •

Sometimes elephants rest their trunks on their tusks, because they're so heavy.

• • •

On average, elephants produce around 80 lbs. (36 kg) of poop a day.

African elephants.

African elephants.

Every elephant's ears are unique — they can be used to identify them, just like human fingerprints.

• • •

There are around 35,000 Asian elephants living across 13 Southeast Asian countries, including India and Thailand.

• • •

Elephants walk on their toes.

Elephant calves have milk tusks, which fall out when they are around one year old.

• • •

Most female Asian elephants never grow tusks.

• • •

Scientists who study elephants are called **elephantologists**.

• • •

Elephants and humans are the only known species to have death rituals when someone dies.

An Asian elephant in Thailand.

When a solitary elephant loses its last set of teeth they will often die, as they will no longer be able to chew and consume food, leading to starvation. However, elephants who are part of a herd are more likely to survive, as they can rely on the help of other herd members to find and gather food, or even to chew it for them.

• • •

Although most elephants have five toes, they don't always have five toenails — most only have four.

Elephants can sleep while standing up. They have a unique ability to lock their legs, which allows them to remain standing while they take a nap. This is especially useful for wild elephants, as it allows them to stay alert and responsive to potential threats while they are resting. Elephants can also sleep while lying down, but they tend to do so for shorter periods of time

• • •

Elephants show a huge range of emotions, just like humans, including grief, happiness, humor and cooperation.

African elephants.

Elephant trunks are sensitive enough to be able to pick up a single blade of grass.

• • •

Elephants are famous for their amazing memories. Studies have shown that elephants can recognize other elephants they haven't seen in decades.

• • •

Elephant calves can't use their trunks straight away, it takes a few months before they can control it.

An Asian elephant family   >

An African elephant keeping his eye on a zebra.

Elephants in the wild spend huge amounts of their lives walking around, so ones that are kept in zoos often have problems with their feet.

• • •

Elephants have been domesticated for thousands of years. Just like horses in many cultures, elephants are used for carrying heavy loads and taking people places.

• • •

The older an elephant gets, the less it sits down. This is because it gets much harder for them to get up again!

African elephants can make a wide range of noises including purrs, grunts, whistles and trumpeting.

• • •

Despite what most people think, elephants don't like peanuts.

• • •

The elephant's closest relatives are the hyrax, the aardvark and the manatee.

• • •

Fossil records show that there have been over 170 different species of elephants living on Earth throughout history.

An African elephant.

An African elephant.

Until 2010, scientists thought there were only two species of elephants — African and Asian, but as you know, there are now three: Asian, African forest and African bush elephants.

• • •

When elephants leave holes in the ground from their heavy feet, they create small water holes for other animals.

• • •

When elephants walk through tall grass, it helps birds to find food as it disturbs small reptiles and insects.

In the Hindu religion, the god Ganesha has an elephant head. Ganesha represents intellect and wisdom.

• • •

We all know that elephants are smart, but did you know that they can draw and play musical instruments?

• • •

A blue whale's tongue is the same size and weight as a full-grown African elephant.

An Asian elephant
cooling itself down.

A young
Asian
elephant.

Elephants are one of the few animals that can die of a broken heart. When a herd's matriarch dies, the remaining elephants in the herd will often become visibly distressed and may stop eating and drinking. This can lead to their death if they do not receive proper care.

• • •

You can work out an elephant's height from the size of its footprint. The footprint can also tell you the age of the elephant.

• • •

Some elephants snore when they sleep!

ELEPHANT
CONSERVATION

Unfortunately, elephants face many problems. They're being poached for their ivory at an alarming rate — it's estimated that around 20,000 elephants are killed illegally each year just for their tusks. This has caused a massive drop in elephant populations. African elephants have decreased by 30% in just the past seven years and Asian elephants have seen a 50% decrease in population over the past century.

And it's not just poaching; habitat destruction is also a big problem. With more and more human development and expansion, elephants are losing their natural habitats and it's becoming harder for them to find food and a place to call home.

Climate change is also playing a part in making things harder for them. All of these problems have led to elephants being classified as "endangered" on the IUCN Red List, so it's up to us to do what we can to help protect these amazing creatures.

HOW CAN YOU HELP?

There are lots of ways in which you can help protect the future of elephants. Organizations such as the **World Wildlife Fund** and the **African Elephant Specialist Group** are dedicated to the conservation of elephants and their habitats. However, you don't have to be a scientist to help elephants. We can all play a role in protecting these amazing creatures and their habitat.

JUST A FEW WAYS YOU CAN HELP:

- Adopt or sponsor an elephant;
- Raise funds for elephant conservation projects in your community or school;
- On special occasions, ask for donations to elephant conservation organizations in your name instead of gifts;
- Spread awareness through social media and educate your friends and family about the challenges elephants face;
- Reducing energy consumption, recycling, and reducing meat consumption can all help combat climate change, which affects the elephant's habitat.

International Elephant Day, celebrated on August 12th, is another excellent opportunity to raise awareness and support for these animals.

ELEPHANT QUIZ

Now test your knowledge in our Elephant Quiz! Answers are on page 83.

1   Can you name the three species of elephants?

2   Which is the biggest species of elephant?

3   Elephants are carnivores. True or false?

4   Do elephants have better eyesight or sense of smell?

5   How much water can elephants drink in one day?

6   Elephants are great swimmers. True or false?

7   How many muscles are in an elephant's trunk?

8   How do elephants cool themselves down?

9   How far away can an elephant smell water?

10   How long can elephants live for?

11   What is the average walking speed of an elephant?

12   How thick is an elephant's skin?

ANSWERS

1. African bush, African forest, Asian

2. African bush elephant.

3. False.

4. Sense of smell.

5. 80 gallons (300 litres).

6. True.

7. More than 40,000.

8. By flapping their ears.

9. From three miles away.

10. Elephants can live to be over 70 years old.

11. 4 mph (6.4 km/h).

12. It is one inch (2.5 cm) thick.

13. 22 months.

14. August 12th.

15. Ganesha.

16. The hyrax, the aardvark and the manatee.

17. An elephantologist.

18. A herd.

19. Elephants.

20. Calves.

Elephant
WORD SEARCH

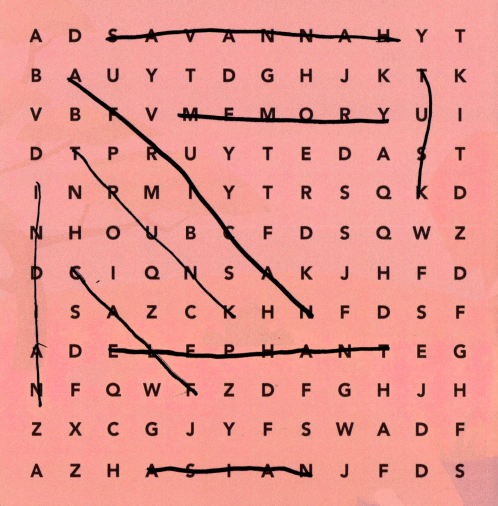

```
A  D  S  A  V  A  N  N  A  H  Y  T
B  A  U  Y  T  D  G  H  J  K  T  K
V  B  F  V  M  E  M  O  R  Y  U  I
D  T  P  R  U  Y  T  E  D  A  S  T
I  N  P  M  I  Y  T  R  S  Q  K  D
N  H  O  U  B  C  F  D  S  Q  W  Z
D  G  I  Q  N  U  S  A  K  J  H  D
I  S  A  Z  C  K  H  N  F  D  S  F
A  D  E  L  E  P  H  A  N  T  E  G
N  F  Q  W  F  Z  D  F  G  H  J  H
Z  X  C  G  J  Y  F  S  W  A  D  F
A  Z  H  A  S  I  A  N  J  F  D  S
```

Can you find all the words below in the word search puzzle on the left?

SOLUTION

		S	A	V	A	N	N	A	H	
	A									T
		F		M	E	M	O	R	Y	U
	T		R							S
I	R		I							K
N		U		C						
D	C		N		A					
I		A		K		N				
A	E	L	E	P	H	A	N	T		
N			F							
		A	S	I	A	N				

SOURCES

"Elephant | Description, Habitat, Scientific Names, Weight, & Facts". 2023. Encyclopedia Britannica. https://www.britannica.com/animal/elephant-mammal.

"African Forest Elephant | Mammal". 2023. Encyclopedia Britannica. https://www.britannica.com/animal/African-forest-elephant.

"Asian Elephant | Species | WWF". 2023. World Wildlife Fund. https://www.worldwildlife.org/species/asian-elephant.

"Asian Elephants: Highly Intelligent Caretakers Of The Southeast Jungles | One Earth". 2023. One Earth. https://www.oneearth.org/species-of-the-week-asian-elephant/.

"African Savanna Elephant | Species | WWF". 2023. World Wildlife Fund. https://www.worldwildlife.org/species/african-savanna-elephant.

"Our Top 10 Facts About Elephants". 2023. WWF. https://www.wwf.org.uk/learn/fascinating-facts/elephants.

"13 Fascinating Facts About Elephants". 2023. Treehugger. https://www.treehugger.com/facts-change-way-see-elephants-4869315.

"10 Amazing Elephant Facts You Need To Know - United For Wildlife". 2023. United For Wildlife. https://unitedforwildlife.org/news/10-amazing-elephant-facts-need-know/.

"Home - Elephant Conservation Center". 2023. Elephant Conservation Center. https://www.elephant-conservationcenter.com/.

Buffalo, Built. 2023. "About Elephants | Elephant Conservation &Amp; Protection". Sheldrick Wildlife Trust. https://www.sheldrickwildlifetrust.org/about/species-we-protect-elephants.

We hope you learned some awesome facts about elephants!

We'd love to hear your opinion in a review. Not only do they make us smile, but they help others choose which books to buy.

Visit us at www.bellanovabooks.com for more great books.

ALSO BY JENNY KELLETT

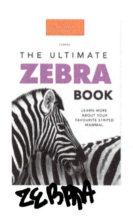

ZEBRA

SNOW LEOPARD

PANDA

MEERKAT

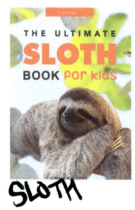

SLOTH

RABBIT

... and more!

Printed in the USA
CPSIA information can be obtained
at www.ICGtesting.com
LVHW070938121123
763707LV00023B/1220